BRITISH RAILWAYS

PAST and PRESENT

No 46

London { Charing Cross } —to

Passenger Luggage.

68

Passenger Luggage.

Folkestone
Harbour.

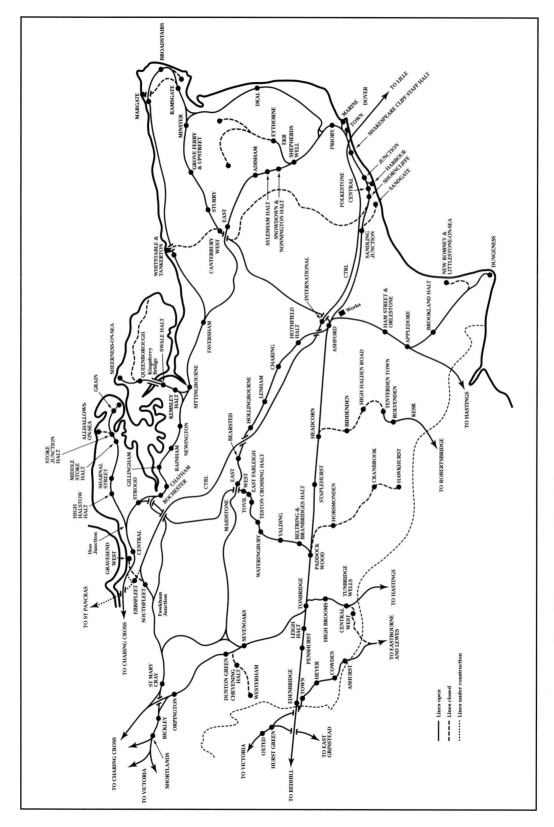

Map of the area covered by this book, showing locations featured or referred to in the text.

BRITISH RAILWAYS

PAST and PRESENT

No 46

Kent

Terry Gough

Past and Present

Past & Present Publishing Ltd

First published in 2004

British Library Cataloguing in Publication Data

A catalogue record for this book is available from the British Library.

ISBN 1 85895 238 7

Past & Present Publishing Ltd
The Trundle
Ringstead Road
Great Addington
Kettering
Northants NN14 4BW

Tel/Fax: 01536 330588
email: sales@nostalgiacollection.com
Website: www.nostalgiacollection.com

Printed and bound in Great Britain

All photographs were taken by the author unless otherwise credited, and all items of ephemera are from the author's collection.

LENHAM is on the line from Ashford to Maidstone East. On 28 March 1961 preparation is in progress for re-instating a loop behind the up platform as Class 4MT No 80017 approaches the station with the 12.02pm Ashford to Maidstone West train.

The view is now more restricted and the embankment overgrown, which makes the bridge look much smaller. In the summer of 2003 the VSOE ran several times between London and Folkestone; on most occasions the train was top-and-tailed, in this instance the rear locomotive being Class 37 No 37065.

CONTENTS

BIBLIOGRAPHY

Gough, Terry *British Railways Past & Present No 45, Sussex* (Past & Present Publishing, 2004) ISBN 1 85895 239 5

British Railways Past & Present Companion: The Kent & East Sussex Railway (Past & Present Publishing, 1998) ISBN 1 85895 149 6

Rediscovering Railways, West Sussex (Past & Present Publishing, 2002) ISBN 1 85895 212 3

The Southern Railway Collection: Kent and Sussex (Silver Link Publishing, 2004) ISBN 1 85794 127 6

The Southern Railway Collection: Branch Lines Recalled (Silver Link Publishing, 1999) ISBN 1 85794 126 8

Morrison, Brian and Beer, Brian *British Railways Past & Present No 20, Kent and East Sussex* (Past & Present Publishing, 1994) ISBN 1 85895 044 9

PENSHURST has changed significantly since Class 4MT No 80013 arrived on the 12.40pm Tonbridge to Redhill train on 19 May 1961. The level crossing has been closed and the line can only be crossed by footbridge, while the platforms are no longer staggered and the original buildings have been demolished. On 24 April 2003 two Class 508 EMUs pass: on the left is No 508201 forming the 16.57 London Bridge to Tonbridge service, and on the right No 508202 is the 17.43 Tonbridge to Redhill service.

INTRODUCTION

The two major railway companies in Kent were the London, Chatham & Dover Railway (LCDR) and the South Eastern Railway (SER), which joined forces at the turn of the 20th century to form the South Eastern & Chatham Railway (SECR). This became the Eastern Section of the Southern Railway in 1923, and of British Railways Southern Region in 1948. Following privatisation of the railways, the train operating company responsible for almost all services in Kent from 1996 was Connex, but the company did not perform as had been hoped and the franchise was terminated in November 2003. Operations were then taken over by South Eastern Trains, under the Strategic Rail Authority. There were also independent railways in Kent, notably the East Kent Railway, serving the collieries south of Canterbury, and the Kent & East Sussex Railway, in the hop-growing area around Tenterden, the purpose of which was not so obvious. Parts of both are now operated as heritage lines.

There are two main lines through Kent from London, one from Victoria (LCDR) through the Medway towns and into North and East Kent to Dover. The other is from Charing Cross (SER) through Tonbridge and Ashford to Dover. Tonbridge is the junction for the main line to Hastings, which beyond Tunbridge Wells runs in East Sussex. There is an extensive outer suburban network, most of which was electrified in the late 1930s. There are secondary routes radiating from Ashford, to Maidstone, Ramsgate via Canterbury, and Hastings, all of which remain open. Branches to Sheerness-on-Sea and Maidstone are also still active. There were several other branch lines, including the Elham Valley, Gravesend West, Westerham, Hawkhurst, Allhallows-on-Sea and New Romney, and these are all closed to passengers, although the latter two are still open in part for freight traffic. Apart from stations on the above lines, there have been few station closures; these include, in chronological order, are Smeeth, Teston Crossing Halt, Hothfield Halt, Folkestone Junction and Grove Ferry & Upstreet. The line running east from Tunbridge Wells into former London, Brighton & South Coast Railway territory has also closed to regular traffic, but is operated by the Spa Valley Railway as far as Groombridge. Kent has recently seen the opening of a new railway, the high-speed rail link from the continent to London, known as the Channel Tunnel Rail Link (CTRL).

The electrified lines of the Southern Railway from the suburban area reached as far as Sevenoaks on the Dover main line and Gillingham on the North Kent line. The secondary route from London to Ashford was electrified as far as Maidstone East. A major extension of electrified lines had been planned by the Southern Railway, but was not implemented until BR days. The first phase was from Gillingham to Faversham, Ramsgate and Dover, including the Sheerness-on-Sea branch, and this took place in 1959. The second phase covered the main line from Sevenoaks to Tonbridge, Ashford and Dover, the Ramsgate lines from both Dover and Ashford, and the lines to Maidstone East and West. This was scheduled for completion in 1962, but much of the work was completed ahead of time and electric trains began running a year early. The Hastings line had been dieselised in 1957 and was electrified in 1986. Tonbridge to Redhill was electrified in 1994 in preparation for frequent electric locomotive-hauled freight trains to the Channel Tunnel, which never materialised. Trains are currently operated by South Eastern Trains, with a small number by Southern (formerly Network South Central). This includes the only passenger line in Kent still diesel-operated, that between Ashford and Hastings, known as the Marshlink. Passenger trains operated by Eurostar started running in 1994 between Waterloo and Paris/Brussels using existing electrified lines, and it was not until 2003 that the first section of the CTRL through Kent was opened.

In the early BR period, the main lines saw SR-built 'Pacifics' and 'King Arthurs' on the express trains and SECR and SR 4-4-0s on the lesser trains. Rolling-stock was predominantly of pre-war SR and pre-Grouping origin. The branch lines were worked mostly by SECR Class 'H' 0-4-4 tank engines and ancient push-pull-fitted coaches. Electric services were worked by SR-built stock. All this changed very quickly with the extension of electrification, hastened by the temporary use of diesel locomotives. The new electric units (mostly Class 4-CEP) were based on what are now known as BR Mark I slam-door coaches. Improvements in frequency and journey times were dramatic; for example, there were 14 steam trains from Charing Cross to Dover Priory, and this almost doubled to 26 on electrification, while the journey time from Victoria to Margate was reduced by 20 minutes. Expectations have risen over the years and present-day travellers do not regard these units as particularly fast or comfortable. Secondary lines were provided with units of Class 2-HAP, which have since been replaced by other Mark I stock (4-VEPs) and by Class 508 units originally built in 1979 for inner suburban services. Other modern stock commonly seen in Kent are 'Networkers' of Class 465, which were built between 1991 and 1993 for Kent Coast services. The last of the Mark I stock is in the process of being withdrawn and new express units of Class 375 ('Electrostars') were being introduced as this book went to press. On the only DMU-operated line, new units to replace late-1950s stock arrived at the end of May 2004.

These modern units and Eurostar trains provide Kent with some of the most up-to-date rolling-stock in the country. However, the Strategic Rail Authority's proposals for integrated rail services with a single train-operating company throughout Kent, if adopted, will not give rise to improvements for all rail travellers. Proposals include the running of domestic services on part of the CTRL to improve journey times between London and the Medway towns, Ashford, Folkestone and the Isle of Thanet. Stations serving some smaller communities would fare very badly, in one case frequency of trains being reduced from 20 trains per day in each direction to one *per week*.

There is a significant amount of non-passenger traffic in Kent, including cars, containers, china clay, nuclear waste, stone and, until recently, mail and scrap metal. There is cross-Channel traffic, but not as high as originally forecast. Trains are operated by English, Welsh & Scottish Railways (EWS), Freightliner, GB Railfreight, Direct Rail Services (DRS), and Eurotunnel.

Virtually all locations visited for both the 'past' and 'present' photographs were reached by public transport, where necessary walking from the nearest station or bus stop. Covering a county remote from home has its drawbacks, as repeat visits are time-consuming; on one occasion I travelled to the closed station of Grove Ferry & Upstreet for a special train, only to have my view blocked by an EMU travelling in the opposite direction. On a visit to Grain, I inadvertently chose the day that most freight trains were cancelled. Despite this, the experience, as always, was enjoyable, and it is hoped that the reader will also gain some pleasure from studying the photographs.

Terry Gough, Sherborne

ACKNOWLEDGEMENTS

The author thanks the various photographers who have kindly loaned him material for this book. British Railways provided a lineside pass, which gave access to the locations for the 'past' photographs. The majority of locations for the 'present' photographs are accessible to the public, but for those locations on private land, the author is grateful for permission to enter. Colin Pattle and Dick Ware are thanked for providing information on current practice The author also thanks his wife, who accompanied him on several of the steam era visits, but decided to remain in Dorset for the more recent trips.

Ashford Works and locomotive shed

ASHFORD LOCOMOTIVE WORKS was situated alongside the main London to Dover line, beyond Ashford station at the country end. Classes 'H' and 'C' Nos 31512 and 31718 stand outside the Works on 23 October 1955.

This part of the Works is now used by Balfour Beatty as a maintenance depot, as seen on 5 June 2003. The up main line is on the left.

ASHFORD CARRIAGE WORKS: Although by 1988, when the first photograph was taken, the Carriage & Wagon Works were run down, some wagon repairs were still being undertaken. The main line lies out of sight to the left, and on the right is the Hastings line.

The buildings are now used for other purposes and can be seen with difficulty from Ashford International station through a maze of ironmongery. The train on the Hastings line (now known as the Marshlink) on 3 April 2003 is formed of Class 207 No 207202, and will terminate at Ashford International.

ASHFORD SHED had an allocation of about 60 locomotives, the same as Tonbridge, but it occupied a much larger area. It closed to steam in 1962, and following final closure in 1968 it became the South Eastern Steam Centre, but once this organisation left the site it remained abandoned and the building was left to decay, as seen on 19 September 1986.

Much of land remains unused, but some of the buildings (including the chimney) still stand. Just to the left of the site, the elevated section of the new high-speed line to London, usually referred to as the CTRL, is under construction on 3 April 2003.

Ashford towards Hastings

ASHFORD: Class 'O1' No 31048, which was used as the Carriage & Wagon Works shunter, moves a rake of wagons adjacent to the Hastings line on 3 April 1956. The signals for the main line are to the right, and the Hastings line is in the foreground.

On 3 April 2003 Class 207 No 207203 passes the same point forming the 12.24 service from Ashford International to Hastings. Although some of the sidings have been removed, there is still a multiple unit stabling point. The new elevated CTRL runs from left to right, parallel with the main line to Dover.

HAM STREET & ORLESTONE station opened as Ham Street, but was known as Ham Street & Orlestone from 1897 until 1976 when the suffix was dropped. The unique unit of Class 203, No 203001, calls at the station with the 10.13 service from Hastings to Ashford on 8 May 1990. This unit consists of four narrow-bodied coaches of Hastings Main Line stock of Class 6L (202) taken from Set No 1011.

On 20 May 2004, in its last week of regular service, Class 207 No 207202 leaves Ham Street forming the 09.24 from Hastings to Ashford International.

APPLEDORE: Newly built DMUs of Class 6L, for the London to Hastings line, were occasionally used on the Hastings to Ashford services. No 1012 is seen at Appledore on 3 June 1958 forming the 12.05pm service from Hastings.

The DMUs of Classes 203/205 and 207, referred to as 'Thumpers', were due to be replaced by new DMUs from May 2004. Immediately prior to the introduction of the Summer 2004 timetable, just one of the new Class 170 units built for the Marshlink was in use. This is No 170726 on the 10.24 service from Hastings to Ashford International on 20 May. Conductor rails have been laid in the siding; these are not a remnant of the abandoned plan to electrify the line, but are used by the adjacent railway maintenance training unit.

The normal locomotives on this line were Class 'H' tank engines, and on the same day in 1958 No 31279 works the 1.00pm train from New Romney to Hastings.

BROOKLAND HALT: Another Class 'H' on a New Romney train, this time No 31521, leaves Brookland Halt on the 10.10am from Ashford on 5 September 1956. The branch closed to passengers in 1967, but has been retained for traffic to Dungeness Power Station.

On 1 July 2003 two Class 20s Nos 20312 and 20313 take a nuclear flask train from Sellafield past the site of the halt.

Kent & East Sussex Line

HEADCORN: Class 'A1X' No 2640 shunts on the KESR line at Headcorn in the late 1940s. The KESR station is behind the camera.

Nothing now remains and most of the site has returned to nature. However, a freight loop now passes through part of the KESR station site, and is seen on 27 May 2004. The train on the right is the 13.52 Ashford International to Charing Cross, which has a scheduled 8-minute stop at Headcorn to allow a fast train to London to pass, and to enable the author to take the 'present' photograph!

Lens of Sutton/TG

K. & E. S. RLY.
Soldiers or Sailors in Uniform
CHEAP TICKET
Headcorn Jnct.
TO
High Halden Rd
Fare **6**d
Outward Half
Not Transfer ble

K. & E. S. RLY.
Soldiers or Sailors in Uniform
CHEAP TICKET
High Halden Road
TO
HEADCORN JUNCTION
Fare **6**d
Return Half
Not Transferable

1762

1762

BIDDENDEN: Looking toward Tenterden in the early 1950s, Class 'O1' No 31064 heads the usual single-coach train to Headcorn. The station building has since been extended and converted into a private house, and parts of the platform remain. *Lens of Sutton/TG*

HIGH HALDEN ROAD: Another Class 'O1', this time on a Tenterden train, crosses the road immediately beyond High Halden station. The same location is easily recognisable today, as the station still stands. *Lens of Sutton/TG*

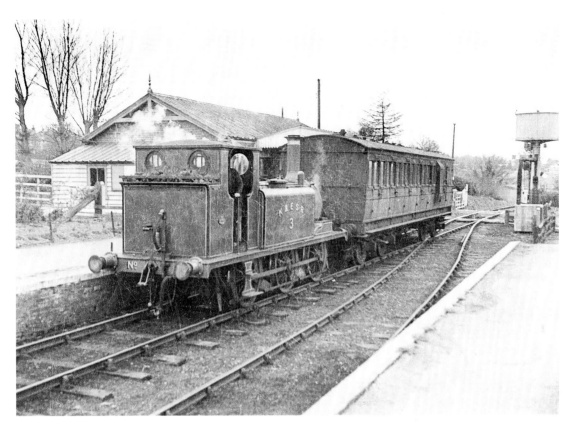

TENDERDEN TOWN: In the days before the KESR became part of the Southern Region of BR, Class 'A1X' No 3 (formerly LBSCR No 70) has just ascended the bank from Rolvenden and entered Tenterden Town station.

The engine is still on the railway today as BR No 32670. This station is very much alive and is the eastern terminus of the present KESR and headquarters of the Tenterden Railway Company. *Lens of Sutton/TG*

ROLVENDEN: Class '0395' No 30576 shunts at Rolvenden, the original headquarters of the KESR. This engine, built by the LSWR in 1883 as No 440, was withdrawn in 1951. The site now includes both a station and locomotive depot, and in the summer of 1996 a train from Tenterden to Northiam enters the station. *Lens of Sutton/TG*

Hawkhurst branch

PADDOCK WOOD: Class 'C' No 31256 is in the Hawkhurst bay platform at Paddock Wood on 10 June 1961. On the far right, in the bay, a new 2-HAP unit waits to take over on the first day of the electric service to Maidstone West in two days' time.

Part of the Hawkhurst bay still exists, but most of the area is a car park. The Maidstone West bay is still in regular use (see page 26).

HORSMONDEN: This branch was also usually worked by Class 'H' tank engines, but on 10 June 1961, the last day of services, Class 'C' No 31588 took the 1.05pm train from Hawkhurst to Paddock Wood, with Set 609.

Since closure, the station buildings have been extended and the site is currently used for a car repair business.

CRANBROOK: On the day after closure to regular services, a special working from Victoria was hauled along the Hawkhurst branch by Class 'O1' No 31065 and Class 'C' No 31592. The train is seen leaving Cranbrook.

Cranbrook station and yard are both still in use, as a private house and gas depot respectively. The course of the line can be seen from the nearby bridge even after a gap of 42 years. The roof of the station house is just visible.

HAWKHURST: The branch pick-up freight was worked for years by a Class 'C', but at the beginning of 1958 a diesel shunter, No D3467, was used on a trial basis, and is seen shunting at Hawkhurst on 4 February. The use of diesels was soon abandoned and a Class 'C' was re-instated until closure of the line.

The station yard is now used by several small industrial companies. The signal box and goods shed still stand and are both in good repair.

Paddock Wood to Maidstone West

PADDOCK WOOD: On 9 September 1988 the Maidstone bay contains Class 416 (2-EPB) No 6406. On the left, recently withdrawn Hastings Unit No 1018 awaits it fate.

Maidstone trains are now normally worked by Class 508 EMUs, such as No 508211 arriving with the 17.35 service from Strood on 5 June 2003. Despite the overgrown nature of the goods yard, it is still open and has a train twice a week.

BELTRING & BRANBRIDGES HALT: This attractive halt, with its traditional wooden platforms, is seen on 18 September 1960.

The halt is still open today and all trains stop here, although there is a proposal to reduce this to one train each way *per week*. On 27 July 2003 Class 508 No 508202, forming the 17.00 service from Paddock Wood to Strood, has just picked up a few passengers. The platforms have been rebuilt and lengthened.

YALDING: On 6 April 1960 the 5.42pm from Paddock Wood to Maidstone West consists of push-pull Set No 609 and Class 'H' No 31517, seen here at Yalding.

In the early years following electrification, Classes 2-EPB and 2-HAP were normally used. On 19 September 1986 No 6402 enters the station with the 09.53 service from Paddock Wood to Strood.

WATERINGBURY: Class 'D' No 31749 enters Wateringbury on an empty carriage working from Tonbridge to Maidstone West on 13 September 1959. The train later returned as a hop pickers' special to London.

The same location sees Class 73 No 73104 on a Tonbridge to Maidstone West freight train on 19 September 1986. There is still a signal box and traditional hand-operated level crossing gates.

It was even more surprising, during a visit in July 2003, to find the signal box and semaphore signals still operational. The twice-weekly freight train from Paddock Wood to Hoo Junction is worked on this occasion by Class 66 No 66017.

TESTON CROSSING HALT: Class 'H' No 31164 pauses at the halt with the 2.04pm Sevenoaks to Maidstone West train on 13 September 1959.

The halt closed two months later, and little trace remains other than the gatekeeper's house, which is a private residence. A direct comparison is of no interest, as trees completely block the view. This summer 2003 photograph was taken a few yards to the right from the road leading to the crossing.

EAST FARLEIGH is in an attractive setting and, like several other stations on the line, is adjacent to the River Medway. On 20 August 1959 Class 'H' No 31518 with Set No 736 arrives with the 10.32am Tonbridge to Maidstone West train. There is evidence of pending electrification.

On 24 July 2003 Class 508 No 508208 brings the 09.23 service from Tonbridge to Maidstone West into the station. Following extension of the platform, the conductor rail was moved to the other side of the line.

TOVIL station, on the outskirts of Maidstone, closed in March 1943, but the former station footbridge and the boarded crossing over the line are still in regular use by the public. On 6 April 1960 Type 2 diesel locomotive No D5002 (later Class 24 No 24002) approaches the site of the station on a Tonbridge-bound freight train.

As expected, the 15.44 Strood to Paddock Wood service on 21 August 2003 was formed of a Class 508 EMU, in this instance No 508211.

MAIDSTONE WEST: Class 'Q1' No 33033 passes with a freight train from Tonbridge as EMU No 5604 waits to begin its short journey to Strood on 6 April 1960. This unit was built as a 2-HAP in 1958, and the First Class compartments were downgraded to Second Class in 1976, when it was reclassified as 2-SAP. The motor coach later became part of 4-EPB unit No 5454, and the number 5604 was then carried by another 4-EPB.

On 24 July 2003 Class 508 No 508208 has just arrived with the 09.23 service from Tonbridge, and will return as the 10.00 to London Bridge via Redhill. On the left another unit of the same class forms the connecting 10.04 to Strood.

Ashford towards London

ASHFORD: Class 'N' No 31854 shunts the Ramsgate via Dover portion of a Birkenhead train on to the Margate via Canterbury portion, prior to departure at 10.32am on 26 March 1959. The train will arrive at Birkenhead Woodside at 6.37pm, travelling by way of Redhill, Reading and Birmingham Snow Hill.

The station has been completely rebuilt to accommodate Eurostar services and is now called Ashford International. The surrounding area has been redeveloped and none of the houses and other buildings from the 1960s survive. On 20 May 2004 the 12.39 Waterloo to Brussels Midi service, consisting of units 3004 (front) and 3003 (rear), calls at the station. Since the opening of the CTRL, non-stop Eurostar trains bypass the station using the elevated section on the far right.

Other photographs of the station appear on pages 66, 75 and 80.

STAPLEHURST: 'Battle of Britain' Class No 34086 *219 Squadron* heads the 11.15am Charing Cross to Dover Priory train through Staplehurst on 6 September 1956.

The station was subsequently rebuilt and a footbridge added once the line was electrified. Passing through the new station on 9 September 1988 is Class 47 No 47298 on a down freight train.

PADDOCK WOOD: Type 2 diesel No D5002 (later Class 24 No 24002), heading the 9.10am service from Charing Cross to Margate, makes an unscheduled stop at Paddock Wood on 18 September 1960.

Determined not to stop on 3 April 2003, a Eurostar train heads for Paris as the 08.23 from Waterloo, with power car No 3005 in the lead. Following opening of Phase 1 of the CTRL in September of that year, Eurostar trains ceased to use this route.

PADDOCK WOOD: 'Schools' Class No 30930 *Radley* works an up parcels train from Dover Priory at Paddock Wood on the evening of 10 June 1961.

The modern-day equivalent sees Class 73 No 73131 propelling the 18.10 mail train from Tonbridge to Dover Priory on 5 June 2003; another Class 73 is in the lead. The train returns to Tonbridge late in the evening, but does not call at Paddock Wood. This event has also passed into history, with Royal Mail terminating its use of rail in early 2004.

TONBRIDGE MAIL DEPOT: A few hundred yards east of Tonbridge station Class 'N1' No 31876 has brought its train of wagons from Maidstone West to a halt on the murky morning of 4 February 1958. It was just beyond this location that a Royal Mail depot was subsequently built, and on 23 July 2003 Class 47 No 47732 *Restormel* is on a mail train in the siding serving the depot.

TONBRIDGE SHED is seen on 10 April 1957, accommodating a variety of 4-4-0 tender engines, an LBSCR tank engine and a Bulleid Austerity 0-6-0.

The shed became a diesel depot in 1964, and the area is now used by railway maintenance contractors. Curving away to the left is the main line to Tunbridge Wells and Hastings. The main line to Ashford and Dover is out of sight to the right.

TONBRIDGE: The view under the road bridge at the country end of Tonbridge station on 11 May 1958 sees the 3.20pm Charing Cross to Hastings leaving; it will swing across the Dover main line behind the signal box. An up Hastings train is passing the box and blocking the view of the motive power depot.

The daily 16.30 mail train from Willesden was routed via Clapham Junction, East Croydon and Redhill and arrived either in the up or down platform at Tonbridge depending on availability, prior to continuing to the mail depot on the down side. On 5 June 2003 it was propelled by Class 73 No 73131.

TONBRIDGE: With only a few more weeks before electrification in May 1986, Class 6L DMU No 1016 approaches Tonbridge forming the 08.27 service from Charing Cross to Hastings.

A train of empty open wagons trundles across the junction behind Class 73 electro-diesel No 73112. It has come from the engineers yard, still operational in 2003.

TONBRIDGE: Two trains are occupying the down platform at Tonbridge on 2 May 1958. The front train is the 4.07pm to Eastbourne with Class '4MT' No 80151, and nearer the camera is Class 'L' No 31765 on the 4.09pm to Margate.
On 23 July 2003 the 16.48 Waterloo to Paris Nord Eurostar train, with power car No 3201 on the rear, passes the same point; on the front is No 3021.

DUNTON GREEN: Class 'H' No 31519 propels empty coaches of Set No 732 from Tonbridge into Dunton Green on 30 July 1960. This train will spent the next few hours running between Dunton Green and Westerham on the branch push-pull service; this branch had a most unusual pattern of services, with an hourly train on Saturdays and Sundays, but no service at all on Mondays to Fridays between 9.36am and 4.20pm (see page 50).

Although the branch line has closed, the station is still open and has a frequent service of electric trains. On 5 June 2003 Class 466 No 466001 forms the 08.25 Tunbridge Wells to Charing Cross service. On the down line a 4-VEP heads for Tonbridge.

ORPINGTON: 'Schools' Class No 30924 *Haileybury* passes through Orpington on the 2.12pm train from Ramsgate to Charing Cross on 30 July 1960. On the far left are the platforms used for services from the London termini that finish their journeys here.

On 12 June 2003 the 17.01 Eurostar service from Brussels Midi to Waterloo speeds through Orpington. Following opening of the CTRL three months later, Orpington would no longer see Eurostar trains.

ST MARY CRAY JUNCTION: On 23 May 1959 up and down trains cross at St Mary Cray Junction. The 3.55pm Victoria to Ramsgate is hauled by 'Schools' Class No 30911 *Dover* and the 1.55pm Ramsgate to Victoria by 'King Arthur' Class No 30806 *Sir Galleron*.

Just beyond the junction two EMUs meet on 13 September 1991; the unit on the left is Class 411 (4-CEP) No 1596. *Neil Sprinks/TG*

BICKLEY: 'Merchant Navy' Class No 35015 *Rotterdam Lloyd* heads the 3.35pm Victoria to Ramsgate train, with Bickley station in the background, on 15 May 1959.

Passing the same spot on 12 June 2003 the VSOE train from Folkestone to Victoria has Class 47 No 47789 *Lindisfarne* on the rear; the train is being hauled by Class 59 No 59202. On the right are new DMUs of Class 375.

BICKLEY: Following temporary withdrawal of all 'Merchant Navy' Class engines in 1953, several Class 'B1s' were borrowed from the Eastern Region. On 22 May No 61329 takes the 8.35am from Victoria to Ramsgate through Bickley.

Nothing more exciting than an EMU was seen on 6 June 2003 when Class 375 No 375609, travelling in the opposite direction, formed the 12.42 Canterbury West to Victoria service. *Neil Sprinks/TG*

SHORTLANDS: A down boat train from Victoria to Folkestone Harbour has just passed through Shortlands behind 'Battle of Britain' Class No 34082 *615 Squadron* on 15 May 1959.

Trains cross at Shortlands on 5 June 2003. On the left Class 466 No 466039 forms the 15.08 service from Sevenoaks to Blackfriars via Swanley, and on the right is the 15.18 Victoria to Ashford International via Maidstone East, with Class 375 No 375709.

Westerham branch

DUNTON GREEN: On the last day of passenger services on the Westerham branch (28 October 1961) trains were strengthened and worked by tender engines instead of the usual Class 'H' tank engines; here Class 'D1' No 31739 waits for its turn at Dunton Green. Remnants of the bay platform were still in evidence on 5 June 2003, but may not survive the anticipated development of the site.

CHEVENING HALT: Leaving Chevening Halt on 30 July 1960 is the traditional branch train, the 12.50pm from Dunton Green, worked by Class 'H' No 31519 and Set No 732. The halt itself is behind the camera.

This whole area has completely changed as a result of the building of motorways. The site of the halt is adjacent to the intersection of the M25 and M26, and a road sign can be seen in the background. The site is, however, easily identified by reference to local roads and buildings.

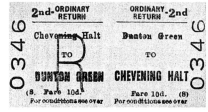

Tonbridge to Edenbridge

TONBRIDGE: Class 119 DMU No L580 approaches Tonbridge forming a train from Reading on 9 September 1988. To the left two diesel shunters are working in the extensive yard, and the main line to London is in the cutting on the far left.

  On 3 April 2003 Class 508 No 508212 approaches the junction with the 16.57 service from London Bridge to Tonbridge.

LEIGH HALT: Class 'N' No 31826 and Maunsell Set No 186 stop at Leigh Halt forming the 9.16am Redhill to Tonbridge train. Leigh was the original spelling of the name, but it was changed to Lyghe in 1917. By the time this photograph was taken, on 19 May 1961, it had just reverted to the original spelling.

The 16.30 Willesden to Tonbridge and Dover Priory mail train was usually top-and-tailed by Class 73s; on 23 July 2003 it is hauled by Class 73 No 73136 *Kent Youth Music*, but on the rear is Class 47 No 47732 *Restormel*.

PENSHURST: Class 'U1' No 31892 passes Penshurst on a freight train from Redhill on 19 May 1961. At the same location on 1 May 25 years later, DMU No L587 of Class 119 forms the 10.39 service from Reigate to Tonbridge (see page 6).

EDENBRIDGE: Class 'U1' No 31893, heading the 1.05pm from Redhill to Tonbridge, enters Edenbridge on 19 May 1961. Edenbridge has two stations, the Town station being nearly a mile away on the Oxted to Uckfield line.

Edenbridge has a frequent service, running alternately from London Bridge or Horsham to Tunbridge Wells. On 2 December 2003 Class 421 (4-CIG) No 1866 forms the 10.52 Tunbridge Wells to Horsham service. Although the siding on the left still exists, it is rarely used.

Tonbridge to Tunbridge Wells
and secondary routes

HIGH BROOMS was called Southborough until 1925. On 2 May 1958 the 3.38 pm local service from Tonbridge to Oxted is being worked by Class 'H' No 31310, propelling a push-pull unit of former LBSCR coaches.

  Present-day trains are rather more plush – Class 465 No 465187 leaves forming the 16.40 Charing Cross to Tunbridge Wells service.

TUNBRIDGE WELLS CENTRAL: Class 3D DMU No 1311 (now Class 207 No 207011) stands at Tunbridge Wells Central operating the 11.15am shuttle service to Tonbridge on 5 April 1986, shortly before permanent replacement by an electric unit. Following closure of Tunbridge Wells West, the suffix Central was dropped.

The Hastings line sees one freight train per day, which runs from Mountfield Gypsum Works to Southampton Docks, and on 5 June 2003 it was worked by Class 66 No 66708. The train consisting of Class 465 No 465017, blocking the view, had arrived a few minutes earlier as the 11.40 from Charing Cross.

TUNBRIDGE WELLS WEST: Class 'N1' No 31878, on the 12.55pm Brighton to Tonbridge train, leaves Tunbridge Wells West on 23 March 1961. This was a magnificent station, but the facilities were far in excess of demand.

The second photograph shows the abandoned station in 1988. Since then it has been beautifully restored and is used, in part, as a restaurant. Most of the site has been the subject of retail development, and unfortunately the same view today is partially blocked by a supermarket.

59

TUNBRIDGE WELLS WEST: The 2.00pm to Oxted leaves Tunbridge Wells West consisting of push-pull Set No 652 propelled by Class 'H' No 31278 on 23 March 1961. To the left, outside the motive power depot, is another Class 'H', No 31162.

The depot is now used by the Spa Valley Railway, which has its headquarters here. The view is more restricted, as much of the site is occupied by the supermarket and car park.

ASHURST: Every weekday evening there were several trains arriving at Ashurst from London within a short time, heading for Tunbridge Wells West or Brighton. On 23 May 1961 'Schools' Class No 30907 *Dulwich* works the 4.40pm train from London Bridge to Brighton. On the left is Class 'Q' No 30537, which will work the rear portion of the 4.48pm from Victoria to Tunbridge Wells West, the remainder of that train going on to Brighton.

There is not much left at Ashurst today, the sidings and main buildings having gone. Trains no longer split here, but there is an hourly DMU and even peak-hour trains to and from London. Class 205 No 205012 leaves the station forming the 16.04 service from Oxted on 5 April 2002.

COWDEN: The 11.00am Tunbridge Wells West to Oxted push-pull service, operated by Class 'H' No 31278 and Set No 656, pauses at Cowden on 2 September 1961.

DMUs of Classes 3H (205) and 3D (207) replaced steam traction on 1 May 1986. Class 3H No 1123 leaves Cowden forming the 10.35 service from Uckfield to East Croydon.

The line has since been singled for most of its length from Hurst Green Junction, and several of the station buildings have been let to small businesses and are in very good order. Canopies have, however, been removed. On 5 April 2003 Class 205 No 205001 works the 10.04 service from Oxted to Uckfield; it had broken down at Hever and is being pushed by the following train, consisting of unit No 207202.

0072   SOUTHERN RAILWAY.   0072
Issued subject to the Bye-laws, Regulations &
Conditions in the Company's Bills and Notices.
Hever to
COWDEN
CHILD
Third Class.   Fare 3d.
NOT TRANSFERABLE.

HEVER: Not all trains on this line were push-pull operated. There were also through trains to London, and on 23 March 1961 Class 'U1' No 31892 takes the 9.55am Brighton to Victoria train through Hever.

The line is still double here and both platforms are in use. On 5 April 2003 the 08.00 service from Uckfield to Oxted consists of Class 207 No 207202. This is one of three units, originally two-car, that have had a third coach added from an Class 411 EMU.

EDENBRIDGE TOWN: This general view of the station is looking towards London on 19 May 1961. Today the yard is used by a builder's merchant, who has retained the goods shed. On 2 December 2003, six days before being introduced on revenue-earning trains, a new member of Class 170, No 170723, approaches the station on a crew-training run from Uckfield to Oxted. These DMUs gradually displaced the 1950s-built stock over the subsequent months. This station has been well maintained and most of the original structure is in place, although the down canopy has been shortened.

Ashford to Maidstone East

ASHFORD: Class 2MT No 84023, working the 2.09pm train from Ramsgate to Maidstone East, leaves Ashford on 21 April 1960.

This area has been completely transformed, but is readily recognisable as the same place by virtue of buildings in the background and, of course, the proximity to Ashford International station. On 3 April 2003 a Eurostar train from Brussels Midi leaves Ashford International for Waterloo on the SECR main line through Tonbridge with power car No 3220 on the front. On the left the CTRL to London is under construction. The EMU is arriving with the 14.08 service from Cannon Street.

CHARING: Class 'H' No 31305 is working the 7.25pm Ashford to Maidstone East train between Hothfield Halt and Charing in April 1960. Hothfield Halt closed in 1959 and decades later the area became part of the huge but temporary Beechbrook Farm marshalling yard (see page 116), built in conjunction with the construction of the CTRL. Apart from this, trees now cover much of the land, providing a contrast with the same location more than 40 years ago. A Class 375 unit passes on a crew-training run on 24 July 2003.

CHARING: Class 'N' No 31868, on the 5.58pm Maidstone East to Margate train via Canterbury West, enters Charing on 21 April 1960.

As with other stations on this line, a footbridge was installed in preparation for electrification. On 24 July 2003 Class 423 (4-VEP) No 3412 enters Charing forming the 14.18 service from Victoria to Ramsgate.

LENHAM: Type 2 Diesel No D5013 (later Class 24 No 24013) and a three-coach Maunsell Set form the 12.28pm Maidstone East to Margate train on 28 March 1961. Diesel-hauled passenger trains only ran in Kent for a short period as an interim measure between the withdrawal of steam engines and the introduction of EMUs.

A welcome change from EMUs on 24 July 2003 is the VSOE train from Victoria to Folkestone hauled by Class 47 No 47757 *Restitution*. The scheduled stop for lunch in the siding just before the station was omitted because of late running.

HOLLINGBOURNE: Most trains were still steam-hauled in 1961, and on 28 March Class 4MT No 80034 enters Hollingbourne with the 2.02pm from Ramsgate to Maidstone East.

The yard has since gone and the lineside is now overgrown. Eurostar trains normally used the main line through Tonbridge, but were sometimes diverted on to this line when there was congestion or engineering works. In July 2003 one such train from Waterloo to Paris Nord is propelled by Class 373 No 3020.

HOLLINGBOURNE: Another engine of the same Class as opposite, No 80087, works the 1.45pm from Maidstone East to Dover Priory in March 1961.

Two of the Class 37s refurbished for the now abandoned Nightstar services tow a Eurostar set toward Dollands Moor in July 2003. The locomotives are Nos 37601 and 37603.

BEARSTED: Another interloper, this time Type 2 (Class 24) No D5017, working the 5.04pm from Ashford to Maidstone East, is seen leaving Bearsted on 28 March 1961.

The goods yard site is now overgrown, so a higher viewpoint was necessary for the present-day photograph. The return VSOE train on 24 July 2003 is headed by Class 37 No 37065. The old goods shed still stands amongst the undergrowth.

MAIDSTONE EAST: On 9 September 1988 a coal train, double-headed by Class 33 Nos 33040 and 33027, emerges from the tunnel at the east end of Maidstone East station. The booking office is on the road overbridge and the station still has its original buildings on the up platform, while new facilities have been built on the down side. A third platform, out of sight on the extreme left, is used as the terminus for some trains from London.

On 24 July 2003 Class 59 No 59202 *Vale of White Horse* brings an empty stone train from Ashford (Sevington) to Acton Yard into the up platform.

MAIDSTONE EAST: The 10.33am to Deal waits to leave its originating station on 28 March 1961 behind Class 4MT No 80038.

   In July 2003 Class 423 (4-VEP) No 3423 arrives at Maidstone East forming the 10.08 Cannon Street to Ashford International service.

Ashford to Ramsgate

ASHFORD: Class 4MT No 42098, heading the 10.35am train to Margate, leaves Ashford on 26 March 1959. The same location is unrecognisable in 2003: there are poles everywhere, mostly catenary supports, and to the right is the new overhead section of the CTRL, ready for services to begin later in the year.

CANTERBURY WEST: A freight train from Minster enters Canterbury West en route to Ashford on 25 August 1960. The locomotive is Type 2 No D5010 (later Class 24 No 24010), which arrived in Kent in 1958.

The overhead signal box is still in existence in 2003. Empty stock to form the 15.33 service to Victoria consisting of Class 423 (4-VEP) No 3554 passes under the box on 15 August.

STURRY: The 11.44am from Margate to Hastings arrives at Sturry behind Class 4MT No 80040 on 25 August 1960. The up and down platforms are separated by the main Canterbury to Margate road.

On 15 August 2003 Class 423 (4-VEP) No 3562 crosses the road with the 13.00 service from Charing Cross to Margate. This train divided at Tonbridge; the front portion ran fast to Ashford and Canterbury West, the rear portion proceeding to Ramsgate via Dover.

GROVE FERRY & UPSTREET was renamed plain Grove Ferry in September 1954, and on 7 October 1956 a coal train, hauled by 'King Arthur' Class No 30802 *Sir Durnore*, passes through on its way to Ashford.

The station closed in January 1966 and has since been demolished. Looking in the same direction from the other side of the line, service and special trains were photographed crossing one another on 15 August 2003; in the foreground Class 421 (4-CIG) No 1742 heads for Canterbury as the 13.30 Margate to Charing Cross service, while in the other direction a VSOE train on a circular tour of Kent from Victoria is hauled by a Class 66.

MINSTER: Seen from the Ramsgate end of the Ashford-bound platform, 'Schools' Class No 30925 *Cheltenham* approaches Minster with the 5.38pm Ramsgate to Ashford train on 25 August 1960. The line to the right is for Deal and Dover.

The Minster-Deal side of the triangle linking to the Ramsgate-Dover direct line is now single track. A vans train enters Minster from Dover on 3 August 1987, hauled by a Class 73 electro-diesel carrying an Ashford-Deal-Margate headcode.

Ashford to Dover Priory

ASHFORD: 'Battle of Britain' Class No 34085 *501 Squadron* speeds through Ashford on a down boat train on 26 March 1959.

So much has changed, mostly in relation to Eurostar, that it is now difficult even to see the station from this viewpoint. This is the view that assaulted the eye in the summer of 2003.

SANDLING JUNCTION has also been variously named Sandling for Hythe and Sandling, the latter being its present name. The 'past' picture provides the once common sight of a Class 411 (4-CEP) EMU on a Charing Cross to Dover Priory train; No 1514 is leaving Sandling on 13 September 1991.

Only a few years later a major change has taken place, and in the background is now the CTRL. On 3 April 2003 a self-propelled engineers' vehicle passes through the station, while on the new railway line a Class 20 heads a works train.

FOLKESTONE JUNCTION: Class 'C' locomotives Nos 31150 and 31004 haul empty carriage stock, consisting of Set No 460, from Margate on 26 March 1959. An up boat train behind 'Battle of Britain' Class No 34067 *Tangmere* is waiting to leave on the right, for Victoria. On the left are Class 'R1' Nos 31107 and 31010, in store after being deposed from the Folkestone Harbour branch by GWR pannier tanks.

On 13 September 1991 Class 33 No 33021 stands in the sidings with a special working. The sidings are used as a stabling point for EMUs.

FOLKESTONE JUNCTION: Class 4MT No 42076 heads the 12.25pm train from Shorncliffe (now known as Folkestone West) to Minster at Folkestone Junction; the Junction station was renamed Folkestone East in 1962 and closed three years later. The line curving in from the left is the Folkestone Harbour branch.

A remnant of the platform has been retained for use as a railway staff halt. Ascending from the Harbour in the summer of 1991 is Class 411 (4-CEP) No 1517; by this time there were no regular boat train workings on the branch.

FOLKESTONE HARBOUR: The 1.20pm boat train to Victoria is being banked out of Harbour station by Class 5700 No 4616 on 26 Mach 1959.

On 13 September 1991 this duty is being performed by BR Standard Class 4MT No 80080, the first steam engine at the Harbour for decades. The branch gradually fell into disuse and a visit in August 2003 found the lines rusty and the station deserted and decrepit.

FOLKESTONE HARBOUR: The 'Golden Arrow' was re-introduced fleetingly (but not from Dover Marine) on 13 September 1991, when 'West Country' Class No 34027 *Taw Valley* ascended the Folkestone Harbour branch on its way to London.

The branch began a new life during the 2004 season when VSOE trains made periodic visits. In previous years VSOE passengers from cross-Channel ferries were taken by road from Dover to Folkestone West to join the train to London, but on 20 May 2004 passengers joined the train at Folkestone Harbour. The train was hauled by Class 67 No 67007, with No 67023 on the rear; it reversed at Folkestone Junction before proceeding to Victoria via Ashford.

SHAKESPEARE CLIFF STAFF HALT: Just before the mouth of Shakespeare Tunnel is a small wooden halt opened in 1913. Most recently it has been used by railway staff working in the adjacent sidings, which were used to bring material to the Channel Tunnel construction site. On 9 September 1988 a Class 09 is shunting a few bogie flat wagons.

The halt is still in existence although closed and in a poor state of repair, while the yard has closed following completion of work on the Channel Tunnel. The up platform is just visible immediately in front of the tunnel mouth. The buildings in the background are tunnel ventilation units.

DOVER TOWN YARD: Dover Motive Power Depot was alongside the running lines at this location. It closed in 1961, but the site was retained as a freight yard. This is Dover Town Yard on 9 September 1988 with two freight trains hauled by Class 47s ready to depart.

This view taken in the summer of 2003 shows that the yard has been closed and the track taken up. Some business has been lost to road and the remainder is dealt with at Dollands Moor.

DOVER PRIORY: Class 'L1' No 31789 collects the stock for the 4.18pm train to Faversham on 24 March 1959. This and the adjacent siding were also used for parcels traffic.

Class 419 (MLV) No 9003, seen in the second photograph on 9 September 1988, was one of ten vehicles built at Eastleigh in 1959 specifically for parcels traffic. They were powered from the third rail, and by battery for use at Dover Marine and Folkestone Harbour.

On 5 June 2003 Class 423 (4-VEP) No 3495 forms the 19.52 slow train to Victoria via Canterbury East. Berthed on the right is Class 421 (4-CIG) No 1876.

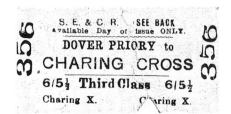

DOVER PRIORY: A Grain to Shakespeare Cliff stone train, double-headed by Class 33 Nos 33012 and 33013, trundles through Dover Priory in September 1988.

Few locomotive-hauled trains are now seen at Dover. However, one daily working until late 2003 was the 19.40 mail train to Tonbridge and Willesden, seen here in the last summer of operation behind Class 73 No 73131.

Dover Priory to Canterbury East

SHEPHERDS WELL: 'King Arthur' Class No 30804 *Sir Cador of Cornwall* heads the 4.05pm Faversham to Dover Priory train as it approaches Shepherds Well in March 1959.

The signal box here has not only survived, but is still in use and there are several semaphore signals on the line. On 14 August 2003 Class 423 (4-VEP) No 3412 passes the box forming the 12.06 Dover Priory to Victoria service, which is fast between Dover and Canterbury East. Little remains of the once busy transfer sidings for coal from Tilmanstone Colliery on the East Kent Railway (EKR).

SHEPHERDSWELL (EAST KENT RAILWAY): The EKR used (and continues to use) the single word Shepherdswell for its station. The line was famous for the Class 'O1' locomotives, which worked the coal trains. On 21 April 1960 No 31258 shunts on the EKR.

Although coal trains no longer run, the EKR is still very much alive, having re-opened in 1995 as a heritage line, with a passenger service to Eythorne at weekends. On 14 August 2003 Class 33 No 33065 *Sealion* stands at the same location, now shrouded in trees.

SNOWDOWN & NONNINGTON HALT was opened in 1914 as Snowdown; Nonnington was added shortly afterwards, but it reverted to plain Snowdown in the late 1970s. There was a colliery here, and on 5 September 1956 Class 'C' No 31255 takes a coal train north through the halt.

The colliery has closed and the rail link severed, but the halt remains open for passengers. Recently introduced Class 375 No 375610 calls there on 14 August 2003 with the 15.11 Victoria to Dover Priory service.

AYLESHAM HALT was opened in 1928 to serve an adjacent housing estate for colliery workers. In fading light, Class 'D1' No 31505 brings the 5.40 pm Dover Priory to Faversham train into the halt on 26 March 1959.

Class 375 No 375610 makes the return journey to Victoria, having left Dover Priory at 17.52 on 14 August 2003.

ADISHAM: In September 1987 Class 4-CAP No 3307 (consisting of 2-HAPs Nos 6060 and 6073) forms the 14.36 Dover Priory to Victoria service. The buildings are boarded up and booking facilities have been withdrawn.

The station is still open, however, and on 14 August 2003 Class 365 No 365511 leaves Adisham with the 16.45 service from Victoria to Dover Priory.

CANTERBURY EAST: A parcels train passing through the station on 19 September 1986 formed of Class MLV No 68003 (later Class 419 No 9003) and 2-HAP No 6087, which is allocated to the Parcels Sector.

This station has also retained some traditional features, in particular the elevated signal box. Class 423 (4-VEP) No 3573 enters the station with the 15.23 service from Dover Priory to Victoria on 15 August 2003.

Ramsgate to Sittingbourne

RAMSGATE: On 12 March 1959 Class 4MT No 42095 pulls out of platform 2 with the 4.25pm Margate to Ashford train.

Track-recording coach No DB 999550 paid a visit to Ramsgate on 3 August 1987, sandwiched between two 2-HAPs allocated to departmental use. The unit in view is No 6022. In the siding is Class 413 (4-CAP) No 3203, formed of permanently coupled 2-HAPs Nos 6003 and 6032.

RAMSGATE: The 5.33pm train departs from Ramsgate to Ashford behind Class 'L' No 31764 in very poor light in March 1959. By this time these engines were not often seen on passenger trains, having been displaced by more modern locomotives. This particular engine was withdrawn in February 1961.
  Class 413 (4-CAP) No 3306 enters Ramsgate from Dover Priory in August 1987.

RAMSGATE MOTIVE POWER DEPOT: Outside the shed in March 1959 are Class 'D1' No 31739 and 'Schools' No 30922 *Marlborough*.

The shed building was closed to steam in June 1959 and modified for use as an electric depot, as seen in 1987. The water tower is the most characteristic landmark. In the foreground is Set No 03, a de-icing unit converted from the motor coaches of 4-SUBs Nos 4127 and 4604. The unit was withdrawn as No 930003 in September 2004.

BROADSTAIRS: Class 5MT No 73085 approaches Broadstairs on the 12.35pm Victoria to Ramsgate train on 12 March 1959.

The platforms have been extended and make this location readily accessible on 15 August 2003. Class 423 (4-VEP) No 3805 arrives forming the 11.30 service from Margate to Charing Cross via Canterbury West.

MARGATE: The indirect but traditional route to London was taken by the 2.45pm service from Margate. On 12 March 1959 'Schools' Class No 30934 *St Lawrence* waits to leave for the journey to Cannon Street via Dover, Tonbridge and Redhill.

The main platform canopy has been shortened, otherwise there have been few structural changes to the building. Class 365 No 365504 has recently arrived as empty stock on 15 August 2003; units of this class did not remain long in Kent, as they were all transferred for use on King's Cross to Peterborough and Kings Lynn services in March 2004.

WHITSTABLE & TANKERTON: In mid-summer, some trains to the Kent coast started from Blackheath, rather than one of the London termini. Here Class 'U1' No 31899 takes the 6.00pm train from Ramsgate on the return journey and is seen here at Whitstable & Tankerton on 3 August 1958.

The extensive grassed area at the London end of the station has given way to a housing estate, which hides the railway line. The only clue to the existence of the railway in 2003 is the transmission mast in the centre of the photograph. The suffix Tankerton was dropped in 1979.

FAVERSHAM: 'Battle of Britain' Class No 34085 *501 Squadron* passes Faversham Motive Power Depot with the 11.15am Ramsgate to Victoria train in March 1959. Note the signal post, just to the left of the engine, with arms for movement in either direction. The depot was at the country end of the station in the vee of the junction for Margate and Canterbury East.

Clearly recognisable as the same place, despite the intervening years, Class 411 Nos 1539 and 1508 pass the depot, now devoid of track, forming the 12.42 semi-fast service from Ramsgate to Victoria on 19 September 1986. A Class 33 waits by the Dover line to bring a vans train through Faversham station, which is behind the camera. The old depot building still stands in 2004.

FAVERSHAM was the terminal point for the 9.41am train from Charing Cross, hauled on 12 March 1959 by Class 'L1' No 31789.

On 14 August 2003 Class 375 No 375623 forms the 10.05 Victoria to Ramsgate service. Faversham has retained much of its character and most of the main buildings still exist.

SITTINGBOURNE: This unusual formation was for crew-training purposes in preparation for the introduction of EMUs on the Kent Coast. Sandwiched between two former LBSCR coaches from push-pull Sets Nos 504 and 651 is Class 'H' No 31512 on 12 March 1959. A Class 'C' is shunting in Sittingbourne yard and in the station is another Class 'H' on a Sheerness-on-Sea train.

The sidings served an oil depot, where Class 47 No 47285 is seen shunting on 1 September 1989.

SITTINGBOURNE: A more conventional sight is this morning train from Charing Cross to Faversham behind Class 'L1' No 31789, approaching Sittingbourne in March 1959.

On 14 August 2003 Class 375 No 375706 leaves the station for Victoria with the 08.54 service from Ramsgate. The small shed on the right is still rail-connected and there was evidence of recent use of the siding.

Sittingbourne to Sheerness-on-Sea

KEMSLEY HALT: Class 'H' No 31242 takes the late-running 11.53am Sittingbourne to Sheerness-on-Sea train into Kemsley Halt, passing the 12.18pm from Sheerness on 2 September 1958.

 The adjacent road overbridge has been rebuilt, precluding a good view of the station, as shown in this March 2004 photograph. Class 508 No 508211 forms the 12.05 service from Sittingbourne to Sheerness-on-Sea.

SWALE HALT: The 11.11am from Sheerness-on-Sea to Gillingham approaches Swale Halt on the same day as the previous photograph behind Class 'H' No 31503. Behind the train is the Kingsferry Bridge, which carries both road and rail from the mainland to the Isle of Sheppey.

A new road and rail bridge was opened in 1959, necessitating a realignment of the railway, which is now higher and just to the west of the original line. On 1 September 1989 Class 411 (4-CEP) No 1563 has just crossed the new bridge with the 17.12 service from Sheerness-on-Sea to Sittingbourne. First Class accommodation used to be available on these services, but currently the Class 508s are Standard Class only; note that headcodes were not in use on the branch. The end of the platform of the new halt is in the left foreground; from here to Sheerness-on-Sea is single track, apart from crossing facilities at Queenborough.

QUEENBOROUGH: It was most unusual to see double-heading on the branch, but on 2 September 1958 the 12.18pm train from Sheerness-on-Sea to Sittingbourne was hauled by Class 2MT No 41308 and Class 'C' No 31269, seen here at Queenborough. Concrete slabs and supports for an extension to the platforms lie on the up platform.

On 1 April 2004 Class 508 No 508205 enters Queenborough forming the 13.56 Sheerness-on-Sea to Sittingbourne service. In the background is a bridge carrying the new road into Sheerness-on-Sea.

SHEERNESS-ON-SEA: Class 'C' No 31112 is seen at Sheerness-on-Sea with former SECR and LSWR stock forming the 3.20pm train to Sittingbourne on 7 October 1956.

The platform face on the extreme left is now out of use and fenced; however, the right-hand platform has been extended and is still in use. Most of the older buildings around the station have been replaced. On 1 April 2004 Class 508 No 508205 leaves with the 15.00 service to Sittingbourne.

Sittingbourne to Gravesend

NEWINGTON was one of several locations where there were changes to the track layout and platforms in preparation for electrification, the line being quadrupled from here to Rainham. Work was in progress on 2 September 1958 when Class 'D1' No 31749 passed through on the 11.45am Sandwich to Gillingham train via Dover.

On 15 August 2003 Class 375 No 375619 is on the down through line, forming the 15.35 Victoria to Ramsgate service.

GILLINGHAM: A down freight train hauled by Class 'N' No 31870 passes through Gillingham on 2 September 1958. On 15 August 2003 Class 423 (4-VEP) No 3454 waits at Gillingham forming the 08.10 Victoria to Dover Priory service, which was running almost an hour late due to signalling problems near Sole Street.

CHATHAM: BR Standard Class 5MT, not long outshopped, steams through Chatham on 7 October 1956. The train is the 10.35am Victoria to Ramsgate, with through coaches for Dover Priory.

Nothing like as impressive, but with far better acceleration, is Class 365 No 365502, forming the 07.55 service from Ramsgate to Victoria on 14 August 2003. There are now only single up and down lines, those on the extreme left and right having been taken out.

GRAVESEND CENTRAL: Class 'C' No 31716 is preparing to work empty carriage stock to Grain on 30 September 1961. The suffix Central was dropped from 1965.
    On 22 March 2003 Class 66 No 66104 emerges from the tunnel on a stone train from Hoo Junction.

GRAVESEND CENTRAL: Class 415 (4-EPB) No 5511 enters the station as empty stock on 1 September 1989.

On some afternoons Gravesend sees several freight trains within the space of an hour, and on the 20 March 2003 the fourth such train appeared behind Class 66 No 66199 on its way to Hoo Junction with empty stone wagons.

Channel Tunnel Rail Link (CTRL)

BEECHBROOK FARM: Large yards were built at Beechbrook Farm adjacent to the Ashford International-Maidstone East line in 2001 in conjunction with Section 1 of the construction of the CTRL between the Tunnel and Fawkham Junction (see page 67). This is Beechbrook Farm looking towards London on 13 September 2002, with GB Railfreight Class 66 No 66712 at the head of a rake of sister locomotives.

Once track-laying and associated works were completed on this section of the new railway, Beechbrook Farm became redundant and was dismantled, as a visit on 11 July 2003 shows. *Both David Staines*

SOUTHFLEET JUNCTION: Further west, between the River Medway and Southfleet Junction, adjacent to the A2 trunk road, earthworks have just started in February 1999. This is the view looking towards Ashford.

By June 2002 track has been laid and works trains are using the line. In this instance Class 66 No 66610 is on the rear of a train of empty hoppers returning to Beechbrook Farm. The high-speed line from the Tunnel through here to Fawkham Junction, where it joins the domestic lines, was officially opened on 16 September 2003, and to passenger trains on 28 September 2003. *Both David Staines*

SOUTHFLEET JUNCTION: The first photograph shows Singlewell, just east of Southfleet Junction, on 13 September 1999. By mid-2002 tracklaying was complete and wiring would shortly begin. Class 66 No 66245 works an infrastructure train on 13 September. *Both David Staines*

SPRINGHEAD JUNCTION: On 20 March 2003 Class 465 No 465248, forming a North Kent line train to Gravesend, passes the site of Springhead Junction, where earthworks have recently begun for a spur to connect the North Kent line to the CTRL at Ebbsfleet. This will form part of Section 2 of the CTRL to St Pancras.
 A visit in May 2004 found that the track had been laid and the spur was in use by infrastructure trains.

SPRINGHEAD JUNCTION: This is the site for the spur in March 2003, where it will pass from left to right and then under the North Kent line across a chalk pit, which at one time had its own railway system; the track in the centre foreground was part of an industrial line in the pit.

In May 2004 the site had changed significantly, with the spur in place and the ground cleared in readiness to lay track for a railhead for construction materials on Section 2 of the CTRL.

EBBSFLEET: A new station is under construction at Ebbsfleet in March 2003, and it is here that the spur from the North Kent line and the new main line from the Channel Tunnel meet, before plunging under the River Thames towards St Pancras.

Much progress was made in the succeeding months and a visit in March 2004 found that the elevated section was in place, although no track had been laid.

SWANSCOMBE THAMES TUNNEL: After crossing Swanscombe Marsh the CTRL will pass under the River Thames, and this is the construction site in March 2003. The tunnel was completed in October of the same year.

Another visit in May 2004 found that the Swanscombe railhead, adjacent to the tunnel, had just started to be used. A former Deutsche Bahn locomotive of Class 211 is backing a ballast train towards Ebbsfleet.

Allhallows-on-Sea and Grain branch

HIGH HALSTOW HALT: On 2 December 1961 Class 'H' No 31530 propels the 1.04pm Gravesend to Allhallows-on-Sea train towards High Halstow Halt, which is immediately beyond the ungated level crossing.

Although the line from Hoo Junction is no longer open to passengers, several freight trains per day pass through on the way to and from Grain. On 21 August 2003 Class 66 No 66502 *Basford Hall Centenary 2001* passes the same point on the 10.39 Freightliner from Grain to Tilbury.

SHARNAL STREET: On 14 October 1961 Type 3 No D6514 (later Class 33 No 33103) works the 1.06pm service from Gravesend to Allhallows-on-Sea in place of the usual Class 'H', and is seen from the station yard approaching Sharnal Street.

This location is now rather unattractive, with a new road bridge crossing the line at the site of the station. Seen from this new bridge on 21 August 2003 is Class 66 No 66230 running light from Hoo Junction to Grain. The electricity sub-station occupies part of the old station yard, precluding photography from that side of the line.

MIDDLE STOKE HALT was opened in 1906, and on 2 December 1961 Class 'H' No 31530 stops there with the 12.20pm train from Allhallows-on-Sea to Gravesend.

Electricity pylons have since been erected along the edge of the railway, detracting a little from the sense of isolation. There is still a crossing over the line by the site of the halt, although the gate has been renewed. On 31 March 2004 Class 66 No 66503 works a Freightliner train from Grain to Tilbury.

STOKE JUNCTION HALT was opened in 1932, and this is the view looking towards the junction for the Grain and Allhallows-on-Sea lines in December 1961. The road to Grain passes over a level crossing immediately beyond the station and before the junction.

Lifting barriers have been installed and these are visible in the background. The line itself is hidden behind the bushes in this 2003 view.

GRAIN: The last regular passenger train from Grain ran on 2 December 1961, worked by Class 'H' No 31324. It left the terminus for Gravesend at 11.37am and is seen here at Grain Crossing.

The area is almost completely flat and most of the industrial buildings, including those of the oil refinery, have been demolished to make way for new buildings. However, Grain Crossing and the gasholder are still major landmarks. On 31 March 2004 Class 66 No 66198 has just arrived light engine from Hoo Junction to collect a stone train.

INDEX OF LOCATIONS